Secret Lives

The Wesleyan Poetry Program: Volume 60

Secret Lives

By

EVANS CHIGOUNIS

WESLEYAN UNIVERSITY PRESS

Middletown, Connecticut

3/1972
am. Lit. Co

```
P S
355 3
H 48
S 4
```

Hardbound: ISBN 0-8195-2060-8

Paperback: ISBN 0-8195-1060-2

Library of Congress catalog card number: 74-185195

Manufactured in the United States of America

FIRST EDITION

To the American master William Carlos Williams
who would tell me that writing is a very human thing to do
and to my father Charles who was a Greek

Contents

South . . .

Going up

blue pampa and blackbirds in the shirttails of the sky
neruda's butterflys galloping against the horses
spiraling mountains of them

i had argued with pablo neruda in a poem about communism
now i believe in better poems

and i believe in giotto
                    and all the lean poets
            the makers of brevity
                            who chew stones

and go in the world just beneath the skin

II
mountains in the arms of mountains
going up to peru

osier catwalks slung between the rocks and lost footfalls
the single dusty lifeline winding out of the navel of the world
the stone city cuzco in a cup of andes city of the blood that if
two travelers pass the one going salutes the one coming away
as his superior

catching a breath in cuzco
                    student of the dust
indios nodding on coca
                    absorbed in dreams of sleep they cannot wake
woodcut shadows in the cold inca square
                where the deadpan cloister bell sounds so loudly out of key
someway removed from the broad central plaza
                            of severed heads and pageantry

[12]   in these smoky asthmatic mountains in the arms of mountains
       we sun ourselves and read the paper over coffees
       the women in their tight flesh
                              swiveling under
                                        shapeless skirts
       high-faced men
                      keeping dark thoughts

       looking among surprising people in unexpected places

       what is there to talk about in this sunlight
       long perspectives through arab arches
       women and blue mountains
       being careful not to talk things away

       dry skills under green eyeshades
       cerebral works that touch nothing go nowhere
       my contemporaries
       full of allusions to allusions make of it all marvelous mechanical birds

       where is the summer heart in the winter brain
       there was no joy in any of them

       these spooked mountains in the arms of mountains
       flames of los andes roped by the neck led in stone silent streets
       the church like a camel humped upon a dusty hill near the market
       startled inca eyes in the candles in the smoke and gold
       a single
                 lance
                      of sunlight
                               pinning
                                     christ
                                         to the
                                               far
                                                  wall

i must make a mass from this torn balcony
i cannot see the edges of the earth and it is just as well
i am without boundaries muerte be careful what you say to me

this is such dark and bloody ground
        the dried semen of history rusts here
                        cracked tombs spill out beneath the city
and there is no public notice of it
                        the public   that was never a cause
on star-choked torch-led cymbaled and feathered nights
obsidian knives gave it over in the name of all the small eye could see

the mass is ended
from the practice of first communion
                        mahogany children pass in white and lace
and we wait to escape into light
                        but escape is nothing
abdication
        il gran rifiuto
                        perhaps that is something

etudes and nocturnes
play among
        the
                broken
                        walls
and through the cold spaces of the southern cross
        radio-astro
                ears
                        hear
                                the death hiss
                                        of stars
                                                traveling
                                the thousand millions
                                                of icy blue

it is time to go up to machu picchu
the old woman and the young woman have made a saddle
in the clouds there

III
toy train working north horses slipping wildeyed on the rocks above
frozen breath and gorges screaming
                                    north through star-flung nights
the ascent followed by the fall
the spilled water by patterns in the dust
                                    pink of breasts on waking

morning in the arms of morning
fleecy cirrus curls round the eagle who excites worth nothing

flights and shadows
between well-couched thighs the sudden mouth gapes speechless

but language is not obsolete
it runs before us in these high thin passes

snow falls upward
and in the far north there is a farther north

or it is only story telling
or gymnastics to wet the sex

sliding by boundless walls sliding by watchtowers that do not watch
at one waystation of the cross there are ponchos spread in the fine rain
                                    potatoes and casavas glistening on them
there is the breath of things growing
                                    there is silage and manure and urine
thrifty nature
            that uses everything changes
        everything keeps everything

for a cityman to be simple is very complex
it is confession and purgatory with the lungs bursting
                    and this naked
                                climb
                            afterward
                                    in the sweet cedar

i cannot tell from here the river furious in my head
if that cloud draped rock is the place
                                    the vanishing point
but i have come through and i will wait here
                        like water
                                dripping
                                        beaded
                                                on this
arched eyebrow of the montaña
            where the high and dry
                        falls
                            abruptly to
                                    the continental thicket

i will mount this saddle in the clouds
                    suck the towering air
                            and give back
                                    blue water

i will throw myself away
                    on these lines
                    and gather up
                            at a different place

American grave

So it was Cortez
and he rubbed the road
The forgerer of history wrote: we were astonished!

One silver foot one of gold
silver and gold foot by foot
adding and deepening six feet down to four across

In went the Toltec in went the Aztec
in went all the Americans
in went cities that astonish; jungle Venices dream Egypts

To silver and gold six feet down
went the old roads and the soul roads
to the elaborate crypt went the cities, and astonishment

In conversation — Santiago

Yes, in Santiago de Chile November rises full of birdsong
we see right off the difference and take off the worn-out climate
walking the Alameda talking of patriots and morality
tongue in groove defining our terms

While in New England full of mauve and brown
waiting for winter to come down out of Canada
the poets and patriots long since beneath the wet leaves

Driving beneath the spanish trees we climbed around
to St. Lucie like an exposed poem in the city's heart
and examined the new day and the old wonder
we spoke of in all those wildest dreams

Coisa mais linda

it is the dusk of Rio shimmering gold of the sea
and blue Corcovado of the smoky soul and phallic
now that two shapes weave and gather stars at the water edge
he saying and she saying licking salt on the face

it is the dark of twilight of this Rio
coisa mais linda yes and he translates into her sea eyes
'a most beautiful thing'
below the Southern Cross and other true altars

———————————

there is in Amazon
that is to say the place without time or memory
a flower beyond intrigue

it reaches and stretches in deep Chartres of green sunlight
that all good men and true and all explorers of the heart know
as the magic mountain and fountainhead

and that flower is you love
that timeless place without times past
the true Brazils

Ate logo, Rio

love like revolution goes to the barricades confident
i wake up sleeping thoughts of you
in the garden of this soul i call Brazil confident of my cause
i pamphleteer and pave the way to a new history

ate logo, Rio
emaciated thighs rise up with the new blood of it
yes until later when you sea dream of Rio emerge
to be what you merely seem to be

as love unlike revolution is without arrogance
i wake sleeping of you
i write my soul full of the guiltless rain
and search my eyes for the new true horizons

Never is a long walk

Never is a long walk alone
and to travel well is to rest wisely
that is suddenly one morning I am sitting on a wooden chair
my feet on the sunny stones below the lover mountains of purple Mexico
reading the mystics of Sister Juana Inés of the Cross
and my rubbings and drawings draining off.   Quite naturally
white birds fly and out of the bell tower the matins.

Back in the crowd yelling Reality!   Electronics!
a rat like a wolf had eaten a child a man ate the rat and all was hunger
and when I looked around the hip and thigh world was slipping away
in its jolly mink sports cars it was making a false clean breast of things
like sex like an ax on the civilized couch and wars for the loveless
as everyone else despaired and gorged himself on ideas and things
on madness which seems now the only sanctuary.
Toy suits and circuses.   Something of terror for everyone.
Comfort and plastic!   All was hunger.

The Big Bang was the earth happening.   Maybe.
But the world occurs inch by inch
and never is a long walk for men to rub against the road to discover
to find out that death precedes life as well as following it
Mexico let us say died to live
and will die again to live again as any other
myriad fat city sassy on the graves of Tenochtitlán gods alive in stone
Friday's worth two million in the lottery   business is holy in neon
though the paseo is performed on the Reforma religiously
occupied men vendors and carpenters are kodaked for posterity
and nothing is removed from zero or what we make of it

I rubbed away and kept my ear to the ground
and I saw things falling of their own weight and kept moving
toward Oaxaca toward plumed Oaxaca I said
'what is a lie but a truth limited by the mind!'

There are well written walls along the way diary of the il literati
vocabulary of the poor short and to the point it's all there
and a well scrawled Viva! gets it said Style is substance
wit reason information aloofness so admired do not get the poem made
as the Monte Alban is a poem
out of the sympathy of Zapotec holymen and madmen
all this dark ground and ruin Mexico leaping with poems
the ancient dead beneath the spanish vaults lament and weave the night
guitars bleed and nothing is removed from zero.

II

I shall write home: To Whom It May Concern
The children are dying!   schooled to death
All that sanitation and no health
The nobility of poverty is not a thought to grow on
I am looking for the true horizon
Leather faces stand by the roadside
There is no Juarez among them   Few saints many martyrs
It is difficult   But the doom of homecoming is greater
Weather is fine wish you were here   E/

PS   the women go bravely   mouth alert   a lot of mileage in the hips
        making what they can out of this still ignorant life

Meanwhile all in all the world's butterfly is waiting
[22] The concrete obliteration to come the internment to come
is not a thought to grow on   The young have arrived too soon
I am looking for the immaculate conception in these terrific scrolls
There is a way yet to go Charro   wish you were here

Of Mexico one wonders
the Aztec valley let us say before calendars [23]
i to arrive across this field of asphodel below the blue gods
alone and full of eyes toward a sea deep wood
where smoky green the sunlight legends are born
where there are talking flowers and a lake like a shy girl
and to no surprise you silky and full of talking rare birds to arise
beckoning with that shy silence that is the wonder of rare things
we to become an emerald quietude there

Gulf coast

This is the muted evening
of which we spoke, wine-colored
sands and sea inseparable, musical
and against the final brass arranged
in crotchets and semiquavers, a profile
of departure. Below the terrace, the nets
and naked yards of the listless boats.

What is it that we see in this
blooming hibiscus of the mind that we
come out of one door and swing through
another with such assurance? Or do we
fall through one to ascend into that other?
How it is, Marius, so assured,
that your city falls away from you?

The palm-fringed violins play
and we are watching the large waterbirds
like flaming swords cut the Spanish gulf
somewhere toward Yucatan.

Well met, San Antonio

Footsteps in the stone gallery down a summer of night
the linden trees released against the black air
luxuriantly composing the ear
in matchless counterpoint.

The girl like a well-turned phrase in speaking lace
entered the yellow arc of the lamps
and was born in the instant of the footsteps ending
and in that first awkward silence.

How do you encounter yourself? the spanish says
and she replied with a throat full of guitars
composing the luxuriant legs
to achieve the ultimate introduction.

We are now off the coast of summer

guano islands like white whales
the prow full of silver fish
and the heart alone

Circling circling the dipping masthead
the clumsy guanera fighting for their lives
in this late century
the turn of the screw that is against us all
dying birds and dying men
staving off obsolescence with one last tack windward

Sketches

It was in a garden of flowery Lima
in Peru at the season of ferias, the
young huaquero voices of the guitars
beating the rhythmic air with flowery
hands. Sun in Lima, that season the
Grand Matador came looking but missed
me at the gate.

❀

You, I sing, Lima
my lips on the white throat of your oceans
when the blood is up and there is nothing
we can not do.

Your white throat beats and your purple sea eyes
beat out the secret codes and lips beat
and the great swells of the sierras rise and
fall gently beneath these my hands
made for rhythms.

The milk of your fountains
not yet dry on my flesh
and you gone into mists so soon.

Lets do blatant things, Lima
like die! and run naked against the sky
and fly like the fat guaneras whose days too
are numbered and dive like sudden stukkas
off the foamy Santa Maria rocks!
Lets get the indios out of the mud huts!
Lets get shot at!
Lets never let go.

❀

At Acho in the night
El Greco shadows on the sand
my suit of lights glows
in the Great Locomotive eyes
in the black bloody mirrors
I see myself

A sweet tree grows
from two silk feet
planted in the cold sand
the sun ablaze at four o'clock
but now it is night
and alone

Beyond the rim of the black bowl
the city lives its separate life
I pull together the threads of mine
one for love one for lost love
an auspicious cartel
and a separate peace.

*

Great loose breasts everywhere!
Go easy, old city, I'm new here.
We feel out the streets
in our Boston walking shoes.
In the Plaza de Armas the adamant
eyes of the palace guard the past
and reflect the neon present
uncertainly. Clothes do not fit
they have a life of their own
the body private and separate.
Like black eels in the Rimac
splashing sunlight right and left
the niños of Lima take their summers

and on the bridge as we pass a soiled
limp rag smelling evilly of rancid oil
and urine turns out to be alive!
A live human form! A terror by Goya!
She must have come with the bridge
a century before, two centuries.
This is the bent corner of the page
that remarks the murder in the gold.

Peru road

I see now the coast road
rag desert and a hint of the sea
low purple hills along the left hand
where beyond waiting and indistinct the Andes!
more a presence a shade a ghost of things to come
down through the villages of Peru the great machine
down through the adobe sunlight we thrusting ourselves
where in a flash on a sudden bluff in a great breath
the Pacific!   leaping emerald wide eyes to see through
you plunge your hand into my steaming chest heaving white surf
and along this dusty high road now at noon there is more to come

＊

I see now the pale sea road
with teeming fish and dreams
below Capricorn

i see now clearly the bend of the continent
that bend of the mind that urges us south

If there is a sail it will be red with morning
far out in the aquamarine mind with pilot birds
and midday rising

i see now the pale sea road with teeming fish and dreams
and below Capricorn would be Chile

＊

Rising
rising wound around us the road
fish to the bait
the moon
the tumult of spring
glassy spring
climbing moon road
and the silver fish rising

Then in this mountain
then in this road this new life
wings filling upward the sun willing
we silver to the bait quick to live

Then all around us night aside day up
stones up bright water lost Inca road rising
this great machine of us uproaring
more to come more to come more to come

Someway

I am sitting someway to the side of evening
composing my skin in rhythmic nocturnes
reaching a singular jawline like the Copacabana
and one agate eye like an Andean lake
The hair of course will rain
Doves will appear pink nippled   A mouth
honeyed and quiet arraying itself unobtrusively
in this floated landscape
And I will hear it all clearly malleus to incus to stapes
and back again along that fine simple line of your thither

Other directions . . .

Secret lives

The george washington bridge is more than steel to cross
this sprung day above the palisades more than calendars to reach
more than dials to set to get where we're going
a boy of six his brother three and me

We are in the dogwooded and blue rocked centuries
to the north of the city by west by moonfall
to settle among the algonkin groves in wisteria trim
by waterfall by random trail to plot the changes

the skin change
                        to let go hope and other hostages
        you to become a stone I a tree
and it is not enough to suffer if we cannot suffer lucidly

I shall become the brave of the fragrant wood smoke
to hear the sap sizzle the green wood whine and watch
the changes of the flames small browned hands sleeping in my hands
passing that unspoken music of the race between us

The mists are rising evolutionary siroccos shape us
and I choose to become this real tree now while there is still time
and to take with me these small animals who are dying out
I wonder what passes before his eyes at three

I know now we will leave together
through the west gate eastward
by the sleeping watchman filled with dreams of flying foxes
beyond the sleeping of the wasps
the smell of the vast continent receding
to follow the wounded sky
where all found things go

the sky retreating to be reborn
relieved of all the luxuries the world enshrines
to a decent respect for life
the life of stones and trees and the great bears
we saw that morning wading through the fogs of Gaspé
the silver fish and the life of the silver wind
and of men as well at last

one man one woman a tree a stone a child
wrapped in their nakedness

Dufferin terrace

We were in the great city of Quebec
the sky an immensity, and below the slow St. Lawrence.
To the south across the townships thick under snow
the long blue teeth of the Adirondacks.
Winter was among us then like some lost animal,
the bell singing brass on the rock candy nights.
And the response offers nothing
like the desire. Afternoons in the green-roofed pavilions,
in summer there would be caleches, kids in bas ville
in the alley streets, the place haunted by moonlight.
Then that summer body that offered everything
and that fair winter face that responded.
All before I would give you up to time and algebra.

Three bodies in Canada

The room
unashamed
with sunlight
reflecting
blue Laurentides
opens itself
to you
for my sake.

Glassy afternoons
plunged in snow
sing our first hope

and we cling to it
for all it's worth
in that honest room.
In angelic light
we slip into night
to sleep the sleep of athletes.

Trail

It is the wine and yellow air of iroquois summer
in these the northern states
                    of mind and substance

yankee arch and protestant

the efficient roadside stands deal in apples
cider jellies maple sugar candy pumpkins
and the moccasin feet drum on the long grass
mauve and yellow the mind expands

the stunned bees retreat into the slowed ground
we go on shifting gears and the great jaguar
mounts the hills loves the hills south toward cities
canada wind singing at our heels

Maine log

I will remember you, April, the long nose
bleak seagone eyes above the jetty
beaten ships at Wiscasset to take pictures by

That sweet lost soul between thighs
of the whitest calm
It all departs to come again

There are others who can build the metal ships
but only the yankees in America could make ships like clouds

Bryant Park

pigeons
      like a tree full of plump tits

panhandlers
        sleeping the same soiled dreams

Or so it seems

Well, he said, it was something
that went beyond politics
Everything important goes beyond politics

And the New York Public Library
in the rain

in this spot George Washington
slumped in his saddle in despair
the British at Murray Hill

walking through there
to work

The colonial cemetery

Under spectral November
shades running purple before the glassy night
beside this churchyard wall crept with myrtle and dried moss
where pathetic legends fade in the damp dolmen
the tumulus cairn and barrow I mend my ways
and salute this well-turned and spent ground

It is a narrow house and the long home
where before these rusted burghers settled in
before the memorial cannon with its silvered spoked wheels was placed
before holidays to the independence of the nation with balloons
were ever spent and bugles attacked the sharp air
I think of the painted braves sleeping against the snows
waiting for the deer to pass

Then that one night in the high air the revolution
cloaked in a great sail in the shadowy wind strode among the stones
everything in the balance crisis at hand
and how the ground leapt up on all sides
man taking counsel drawing a line in the dirt that he would defend

All that part drummed out ringed by blind steel cemented shut
neon replacing the midnight moon that has crossed between this tower
and those bare sycamores from the first luminations
and there is no counsel in stones any longer

The founders for their part
scratched their accents into the red rock and settled in
of the Delawares not a bead not a quiver of any kind
and for my part we stand this nightwatch
to see where it all joins our bones to our skin

High in Manhattan
staring down the sun

(A window desk on the 31st floor above the Hudson
is worth a couple of grand a year)

Inca sun it seems beside the Spanish galleons

the faces of my companion
in stone and gold in a silver brain
                    beside my head

the way he looked on the occasion
                    of our last meeting
before we descended and departed
                    full of winey talk
                    and fiery wings

In those high and endless cradles
                    slung from
peak to old peak we swung through
                    startled dreams

Yet men can only deal with perishable things

Buddha

i spent the day in meditation sleeping in the sun of the world
which is you sleeping in the peaceful sun and the world far away

i spent the meditation of you asleep in the sun's peace
and far away the sleeping world's meditations

now in these sun slept explorations upon the temporal and timeless
i observed a river all glistening with the thousand eyes of life

and at this place departed the one world to enter fully the unworld
which is you full awake beside me above the river of all light

and so we spent this morning which is meditation and bright winds
on a stone ledge side by side with the river listening with great eyes

and then these two of we rid themselves of themselves to enter one self
rid past rid future rid time which is the knife and shackle of the heart

so it is in this spent day of meditating sleep in the sun of the world
they who were separate passed into the oneness of the hearted river

and for all to know hereafter who come this way and willingly listen
the she part is the sun the eyes the stars and he is the sleeping wind

Zero adds up

It was for nothing your childhood
eyes in the rigging of clouds.
You can see that now for nothing the mind
like a blue sail.

In the slow woods the deerslayer on leather feet
crossed the roof of the brain and for nothing
the locomotive eyes charged
the still red mornings.

To be young
in the twentieth century
It was all guile.

We stood about
in our flashing skins
none wanting to be a tree
or a river
convinced that inhumanity
proves man.

Trickery
was the skill
of the age.

Is there nothing but this blind poet
singing the night a cathedral of infinite arches
Was it for nothing the heart
like a lost grail.

It was as it has been
the thing sought is not the thing lost
the word is out and zero adds up to something
The ageless young are rising.

Julia in April

For Julia growing small in April he'd waited
and in the large silence kept working

So it was Easter and April
but we can't wait, he said
and in the large silence kept working
Silky so precise what now of the long hair!

In the antiseptic place curtains are drawn
this is the last and final act
a nun in white walks on cushions
puts her white hand on the eyelids and the eyes close
while back in the lost house a room closes

You see how it is waiting
all those minutes saved
those pins and nickels insurance policies
and in the large silence kept working

And in the large silence working he said
do not fall to the green grass gently

Two women

Walking apace
through the tree filtered sunlight
crossing north of the Plaza Hotel
their heads nod and their hands express the air.

The older one has a professional angularity the
other an amateur roundness. I wonder
if any man can be worth such conversation
and shapeliness.

Tapestry

Hung
          is the single word of its
threaded gold

the window shaped sun lingers along thick
and lush terrains
                    the lute player
hails
      the beauty
of a damosel with one gleaming bare
foot

          and you
outside of it trying to enter.

Cherry garden

It was a Japanese feeling stealing through the air
between you and me and he and them a delicate hand
an every-which-way sun-falling embroidery
a play on words that off-tone broken note
reaching into the moist center like a cry
and declaration for life outside the skin

Blood lines

It is a passion
ancestry.

Among the languid tents where the Rose of Sharon lay
plunged in hot dreams some lean Circassian
was seen to stumble Or was it the shadow of a Mongol
limp on the withers of his shaggy bay?

We come a long way. Clear skin and dark eyes
come through which crack in the holy rock? A satyr
mounting which maid in a play by whom?

What a mastery of intrigue we construct out of two people
lying in the blue tall grass above Mediterranea.

          *

The contessa strolls her gardens above the Abruzzi
dreaming of velvet arms among the dead golden leaves
directs the gateman to the sepulchre each anniversary
to comb the long silk hair of the exposed skull.
And this too is the passion.

Savagery of the blood!
Yet when Homer was a religious teacher
and Aeschylus fresh from Marathon
before going up to Athens to create the world
we sailed off Africa in perfect peace.

[50] **On how one extends
beyond that which
is apparent**

A single sun fed strand of spider's cloth
held so tentatively between wall

and window ledge between time and release
meted out inch by inch

from the beast's willful heart lifts the eye beyond
these summery illusions we choose to clothe us.

Step by step we measure mathematical fate
stunned by each breath

vast horizons filling the sad eyes our windy
heads a storm of rude fortune

compelled by history propelled by hysteria
beyond the reasonable bounds of one sunny room.

Meanwhile the spider without dreams steadily
wills each hour into a silver fantasy

of endless thread that lately follows
from wall to window ledge to bed.

Letter

How clean it is
morning of the world

how lucent the underside of the sealight
thick and silvery with fish dolphin and blue marlin
how clean it is
you morning of the world

letters written in sunlight
to incorruptible eyes from a sea heart

There is a wide veranda facing sunset
passing through glass doors a room occurs thick with life
motes of dust swarming in the last stabs of the day a day passes

there are trees every-which-way against the wind
an underside of lilac on the liquid air tropic air and first star
and if it ends now you say it is a good time

but i am remembering how clean it is
at you morning of the world
and i refuse to close the door

A relative position
in a scale of sequence

now there is a far spot not so far
merely is it perhaps a handsbreadth
below beyond out from the shore of the neck
where the great breast swells and flows
where we listen to the courses of the blood
and count the sprung flights of the tongue

now in this not far spot so far as I can see
which is an unchartered perhaps full of sound
which is the flapping of a winged voice under sail
we'll spend these swift changes
along the long so long reach and infinite eyes
that deliver us into the ultimate flesh

Now country boy

You never ask a jesus place its name
but roll with it and listen to it

the mi god america i grew up in, well
was shot up
and dead or near to death dried out
but i didn't know it

i heard it all love
i grew slowly

this jesus place i grew slowly up in
well i had no name for it

there was the river with no name
mornings full of red fog that was one
and the first place you don't forget
and love it was before growing set in

The go-go dancer

Machine.   All ball bearings and springs.
Fit for our time.
Without brakes.

All arms.   All legs.
Keeping brassy time.
Unrelated.

I see your point / all is lost.   Mind lost.
Go for broke.   All body.
No point.

what remembers best
is the way the breath quickened
and exploded wet in the ear
i'd say

bringing all the wild details together
what unpuzzles best
is the way that casual hand
made itself known

from all that delicious throwing about
what additions best
is the way two things make one hot multitude
i'd say

Patriotism

[56]   (**table talk**)

how can i love idaho?
it's a good sound and an old jazz tune
but more than that?

love country?
yes   what i can reach of it from my porch
through the soles of my feet
the ground that breaks the heart
streets and rain

more than that
just makes no sense at all
i can no more love idaho
than the far side of mirrors
one life at a time, one place

American classic

The architecture of the game is everything
the magic stride
        the arch
            everything
One poem for DiMaggio

pieced out of the public prints
and private dreams summers in the parks
a ball in geometric flight
crowds in the loud stadiums of the mind

The emotional architecture of the game
is everything
        one man
            against a vast sky
A poem for DiMaggio

Hopper

Shadow in light
desperation before the storm
silent painter
of the empty canvas

So, with geometric solitudes
the night hawks live
into the sunday frugal mornings
of somewhere

Clocks and ambush

The
careful
the dutiful
     used to
         pregnant
climates
god bearing god
without end
     little by
        little
withdrew
from public view
and concourse
     finally
        to trust
only in clocks
and
ambush.

Meanwhile
for the brave there was
lucent murder
For those of the true faith
and the underground soul
translucent banditry
and all the great crimes
of enlightenment.

[60]

Crease of joy
            fold of contentment
great rockingchair of night
                        that has beheld these women
at the end of their endless journeys

fled finally that prison of the flesh
now to come this way well-situated
with their crocks and vases full of memory

The whole racked body of men and women to be emptied
as when a visitor leaves the room in which he's been a guest
things to be put in place and the door to be drawn shut

That flash of red
that bird
heads and tails
against the trees the sky
why has he come
all this way
from beyond the Mississippi
to die here
why here?
This is an orchard
where my children play
with faces
each against the day
are children and birds one?
They call and sail
the red bird a brush stroke
the children with broken voices

Later in the huge shade
of elephant ear vines
who will lie down
with Tarzan dreams
what birds will sail our trees
earlier now
each spring?

[62] When two and two got to be four
and the wheel made
all this else was inevitable
white mice sailing toward mars
man on the moon etc.
but all I'm looking for now
is a place to lie down in

a cool wide mind
a place of deep galleries and wide midnights
Tecas in the plains
to be historic in
a place of sombrero moonlights
and lean teeth to chew it with

The chilly ashcan morning

    In the chilly ashcan morning the women
children by the hand entered the broken battlefield;
exploded earth, crippled trees, hung juries, remnants
of husbands.   One child stood to the side with fingers
in her mouth.   A woman screamed.   It was the body of her son.

So, with this behind us, we left the city.
We came out into smudged sunlight on the Jersey side
meadows in a state of high tension and low comedy
and beyond were the blue hills.   We read all the
billboards that promised the Good Life and drove
south on the American Plan.   It was cocacola all
the way.   More money and less wealth, more god and
less goodness we looked for some way back or out of it.

The language was young and we were children
and heaven and earth have passed since then.
Earth and heaven a night change and now
all the terrible infants go
naked in the snow to specialize in ambush.

Peoples heroes

On the funeral of Nikos Kazantzakis
Heraklion, November 1957

The sky was
unending in Crete
The procession
derived from the people
and had no beginning

The books of Nikos Kazantzakis
were carried in the line of march
by young girls in white and black
and boys in black and white

In the wooden box jerked along
in the stone narrow streets
anointed with messages to god and tears
the seamed parchments of the man
come to rest from freewheeling and travels
leaned lastly against the uncreated silence
He could not have hoped for more
though he had hoped for nothing
than this final communion with the wounded hands
and worn shoulders of his countrymen

They put him in the sun-bleached earth of the ruined castle
in high ground which offers views and is a fit place

(At this point, like the stark imaginings of the poet himself,
a giant full of mustachios and old goats steps out of the crowd
with a look that no one dares to challenge and waves aside
the funeral attendants. He is Mamousakas, the guerrilla.
At the time of the Nazis, he was awesome. He is now

retired in his village. In his belt is the thrakias.

He says that only heroes may put a hero into his grave.

He orders the ropes lowered, and Kazantzakis is returned.

Without another word, the old man leaves.

This is Crete which may not exist.)

Note: Kazantzakis had been excommunicated from the church as a heretic.
He was also called a Communist. But the people of Crete buried him
with all due ministrations, because they saw it simply as a matter among
themselves.

Stoop Worker, an editorial

In this minute's worth of hot earth
the sickled form chops out bloodmon
ey Bones etched by a thousand suns
from hell to Texas the skin that ba
rely holds him spoiled for lampshad
es There is a child yet unraped s
leeping on inner tubes and going to
carnivals among the rat gnawed corn
He also had a wife who wandered awa
y. Then there is no hope and if th
ere is still life then there is sti
ll life bent into unlovely moons ov
er coarse fields good for digging u
p the crisp salads that so refresh
those who busy themselves with matt
ers and affairs and trying commerce

Pennsylvania landscape

Coal is what men do.
Coal is God with a black heart.
Then it comes to an end.

The young and the strong run away.
They write in the back of the brain
one word they do not want to forget.

Above the sunken road
lining the tree torn ridge
a row of frame houses

measured to the nail
stare at the world's end
like vacant old men

who have lost one battle too many.
Pale in the fast light these veterans
wait the release that will not come.

Sassoon

Tonight across the news desk died
a relic of the Somme a shade
a poet said the UPI d
of Britain
who had written
a line like a bloody blade
Where youth and laughter ride

Sassoon

Old rebels read the papers:
                          I see where this lady that
died now
            in the newspapers
                        in Chicago alone
was the daughter of the old man
            when they came together
here, which was about 19 and ten, who was the socialist
            and made speeches in the mills
                        until he was put in the jail.
And then the strike,
            the air was full of hot needles,
when he got out and was talking to the workers,
            we were very brave then,
and the soldiers
            they kill him.
                        That was the daughter died.
I remember. Blonde hair. We were very brave. And the father
            always talking.

Sufis, the single-minded

who is to deny them this
heroic ecstasy that asks nothing?

They are not tempted by cash and carry
and turn aside that certain throbbing
for women
and shed their skins

which merely scratch the velvet Allahs
beneath, besides what harm can he do
who celebrates as saint
a poet hanging

upside down in a well reciting the Koran
ears stuffed so the hollows of the skull
transmit
only the oceans of himself!

Silk painters

The Chinese draw their words
        so naturally
           they write
             their pictures

       The signature of a Chinese painter then
is his art and his art his name
      shaping the spirit out of the whole cloth
perceiving the silk of intimacy

    man to man to tree to stone and back
  with the endless eyes
of the rhetoric brush

Columns

The
      doric
           column
of
    massive
          restraint
was
      an
         argument

to the indiscretions
of the excessive flesh.
It
    caught
           the true
greek
      passion
            as that
dia
    lec
        tical and

ancient combat which
confirms the man.

Each
       artisan
             raises
his
    logic
          presumably
in time
      to
          hold up

the roof, parallel yet
irrespective of the others
and
     heedless
             of the fact
that
    such
        columns
are
    designed
         baseless.

[74] The day has a cold sleeve in it
March that titless bitch wired and staved
slips you a tease of spring
then chills it with a mouth full of grief
No. I'll wait

———————

April simile

A sun held thought like afternoon blue
blooms in the mind April offers
as it leaves the skin.

The matchless warm curve of May to come
the blooded woman in her heats
and wiles to come
now alertly and so short time April
to invest the winter heart
like an awkward child

like one brave tree
in a thread
of morning.

May is good for more than desperation. I would not plan the
trip. It should unfold the way a countryside does or a map.
It would happen as the city does or a poem when you enter
them. Stones. Paintings. A symphony. A ballgame. There's
nothing definite. The boys have rung out the rickety bats
and ripe gloves groomed spitted oiled rubbed skinned through
a hundred springs. The click clock of ball and bat and the
slug of the ball in the glove and the faintest whistle of the
ball through the lucid air of this morning. It is a clean way
to start.

Leave something ajar!
Is that a prejudice?
The mathematical neatness of it all
it's maddening.   And worse, it is untrue,
put a chair awry, a vase off-center.
I am prejudiced for life.

Unmade Bed of the Last / or Lost Loneliness

The clear insides
throat down, wind's up in the passes
snow before morning
it's all in the wrists

I am your undefeated
beaten in the hot gates
no good clear lake to run no city of the soul longer
i keep coming back

and i have noted the glorious dead will not forgive
just causes, and numbers are nothing to die for

Yes, the old man
    writing in his delicate ink toward the last end
        the glass of winter it was
    this writing of words, the cracks between
it is a very human thing to do

i wish to paint a giotto poem
for francis

it will begin
firmly implanted in the earth

it will be drenched in sun and rain
and sleep against the snow

and in the spring it will wake and grow
take leaf and become a bird

and in a spear of radiance
ascend into the arch of winds

i wish it to give away everything
and give up nothing

Nature study

She was a woman as glass is a continuum
   offering both object and subject
     a transport of light
      a transmission of light
        She melts into the nature of a room
and assumes the required position.

She was a woman as glass is continuous
offering object and subject
   a transport of light
   a transmission of light
She melts into the nature of a room
assuming the required position.

She was a woman
          as glass is a continuous
offering
    a transport of light
    a transmission of light
She melts
      into the nature of a room
and assumes
      the required position.

Hasapiko

We recall to you gone Helen
of the swept Aegean eyes

barefoot in our dusty hearts
where peeling sunlight lies

a clarinet launching
the swinging ships of our fancy.

✿

To some
dancing is not
entertainment

Pointed voices
search the lost air

To some this
cadence on the stones
is no less than
the tiptoe of evolution
this rhythmed madness
the history of the race
in soft shoe.

[80]   the town was mad for me
but i said no
the town was mad for me
but i said no go back to where you came
from where you sprung boy
they would never believe it anyway in gold
and mauve cloud mountains they eat you alive
but no i said and i tried to make it work
and the town was very mad for me